CROCODILES

Sandie Lee Books

Crocodiles

Although they look similar in some ways, crocodiles are not alligators. These reptiles belong to the family of, Crocodylidae and look like something out of the prehistoric times. In fact, the crocodile has actually been around for about 225 million years! Even though this species managed to survive the mass extinction, some species today are critically endangered. This is due to illegal poaching and habitat loss. Let's explore this fascinating creature to see what else we can dig up.

Where in the World?

Did you know crocodiles can live in fresh, brackish and saltwater? The crocodile can be found in the tropical regions of Asia, Australia, Africa and the Americas. This animal lives in rivers, lakes and wetlands. They are only semiaquatic, which means they spend part of their time on the shore.

The Body of a Crocodile

Did you know the skin of the crocodile is protected by bony plates? Crocodiles can range in size from 5 to 25 feet long. They are olive-green in color and have long pointed snouts. When this reptile's mouth is closed, you can see its lower teeth. It also has a heavy tail and webbed toes on its back feet.

Crocodile Locomotion

Did you know the crocodile can move very fast? Even though this animal has short thick legs, they are very powerful and strong. Some crocodiles can run of speeds up to 11 miles-per-hour. The crocodile moves in a belly run with its legs splayed out to the side in a snake-like motion.

The Crocodile's Senses

Did you know the crocodile has great senses? The crocodile's eyes, ears and nostrils are|located on top of its head. It can see very well at night and does a lot of its hunting at this time. This reptile can also smell its prey from a far distance, whether it is on land or in the water.

What a Crocodile Eats

Did you know crocodiles are carnivores? Crocodiles feed on different prey according to their size, but it will always be meat. Smaller crocodiles will eat fish, birds, reptiles, small mammals, mollusks and crustaceans. Larger crocodiles dine on large prey. Animals like the wildebeest, buffalo and deer can all fall prey to a hungry crocodile.

The Crocodile's Teeth

Did you know the crocodile's teeth are very sharp? The crocodile kills its prey by holding onto it with its sharp teeth and jaws. In fact, this reptile has the strongest bite out of all the animals. The crocodile's teeth also regenerate. This means when one falls out, another grows back to take its place.

The Crocodile as Predator

Did you know this reptile is an ambush hunter? The crocodile will wait quietly in the water for its prey to come by. It does this by floating with just its eye and nostrils peeking out. Once its prey is close enough, the crocodile will suddenly rush out of the water and grab the unlucky animal.

The Crocodile as Prey

Did you know other animals will hunt the crocodile? Adult crocodiles are hunted by jaguars and leopards, as well as large anacondas. Baby crocodiles can be eaten by large birds like the eagle, heron and egret. Man also hunts the crocodile for its meat and for its skin. The skin is made into products like purses and belts.

Crocodile Mom

Did you know the female crocodile makes a nest for her eggs? Before the mother crocodile lays her eggs she will dig a nest in the ground. Some species of this reptile will also build a nest from vegetation on top of the ground. When she is ready, she will lay from 7 to 95 eggs.

The Crocodile Baby

Did you know baby crocodiles have an egg-tooth? This is developed from their skin and helps the babies break through their shells. Whether the baby crocodile is a boy or a girl depends on the temperature the eggs were kept at - the warmer eggs will have males and the cooler will have females.

Crocodile Talk

Did you know crocodiles can communicate through sound? Baby crocodiles will make a peeping sound when they are ready to hatch from their eggs. A high-pitched call is used when these reptiles are in distress. Adult males will hiss and bellow when they are angry or during the mating season.

Life of a Crocodile

Did you know crocodiles can live a very long time? Most crocodiles are hunted by natural predators when they are just babies. However, if a crocodile can make it to adulthood, there's a good chance it can live to be very old. In fact, some have lived up to 70 to 100 years of age!

Nile Crocodile

This species of the crocodile is huge. It can measure up to 20 feet in length and weigh around 2,000 pounds! This reptile can be found around the lakes, marshes and rivers of Africa. The Nile crocodile will eat almost anything, but dines mostly on fish, turtles and crustaceans.

Dwarf Crocodile

This crocodile lives in the rainforests of West Africa. The dwarf crocodile is the smallest of them all. It measures around 6 feet in length. Its body is covered in tough armor and it is black with a yellow underside. It prefers to live alone and will dig burrows during the day to rest in.

Quiz

Question 1: What type of water do crocodiles live in?

Answer 1: Fresh water, brackish water and saltwater

Question 2: What can you see when the crocodile closes its mouth?

Answer 2: You can see its lower teeth

Question 3: What term is used for how a crocodile runs?

Answer 3: It is called, a *belly run*

Question 4: What features are located on top of the crocodile's head?

Answer 4: Its eyes, ears and nostrils

Question 5: Where does the mother crocodile lay her eggs?

Answer 5: In a nest she digs into the ground or builds on top of the ground

Thank you for checking out another addition from Sandie Lee Books! Make sure to check out Amazon.com for many other great titles.

www.ingramcontent.com/pod-product-compliance
Lightning Source LLC
Chambersburg PA
CBHW050801290526
45792CB00008B/2274